Summer Games of Pukatawagan.

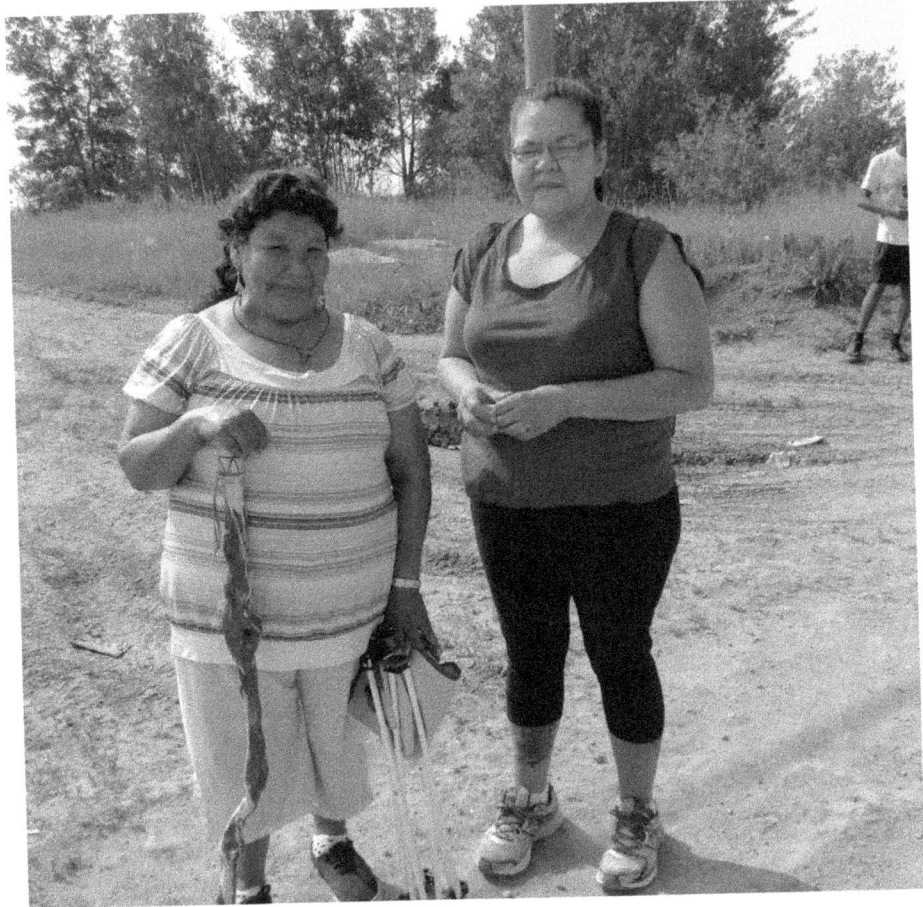

(2 members of Pukatawagan enjoying the events)

(people enjoying the mud pond)

Summer Games of Pukatawagan.

Summer Games of Pukatawagan.

enjoying the events

watching the canoe races.

Summer Games of Pukatawagan.

Summer Games of Pukatawagan.

CONTENTS

Summer Games of Pukatawagan.

Introduction

This book is about the summer games and a brief view on the events that take place. it will give examples of the events that take place from the shooting of the arrow to the paddle and vamp making. these photos and events are just a sample of the games that take place in Pukatawagan, and I am sure you will be interested in participating in one of these fun filled, sweat dripping, heavy

Summer Games of Pukatawagan.

breathing activities.

Summer Games of Pukatawagan.

ACKNOWLEDGMENTS

I would like to thank all those who helped me out with the pictures, without the use of these pictures within the book, it would have not been possible to write this book ''Summer Games of the Mathias Colomb Cree Nation''. and i would also like to thank my classmates at the local University College Of The North located in Pukatawagan, MB and Instructor, for helping me out on Google Docs.

Summer Games of Pukatawagan.

CHAPTER 1: INTRODUCING THE EVENTS.

The Summer Games of Pukatawagan is an recreational event of all sorts of activities such as parades for motored vehicles and bicyclist, foot races such as long and short distance races, backwards crawl, the 1 leg hop race and strength challenges like the boot throw, tire toss and the strong man and woman events, etc. I'll speak about each of the events as you read further into the book.
the summer games held by the community are held every year in the month of august. The summer games of pukatawagan been apart of the community since the treaty days when the members of the band would compete after collecting their moneys. It is also a great time to get the community together whether you want to challenge your family and friends or just test your year's worth of training.

Summer Games of Pukatawagan.

There are some more volunteers
and a few participants that
happened to be volunteers. the
ones wearing the fluorescence
green t-shirt are the proud
volunteers of the MCCN SG.

they help make the games possible
and keep track of all the winners
that participated.

Summer Games of Pukatawagan.

At the beginning of the summer games in the community the shooting of the arrow is the start of the summer games, each arrow is worth $20 - $50 and is decorated.
there are four to five arrows shot every year into the bush from on top of the hill at the local radio station. there are about 50 - 100 people running into the bush finding one of the arrows.
It is a lot of fun competing against each other to find the arrows that were shot into the bush.

Summer Games of Pukatawagan.

Community parade.

(community   parade)

community parades usually take place during holidays such as Canada Day, Christmas and Easter, and during the summer games. judges stand by and give point to the best truck and quad that are decorated nice depending on the theme of the parade.

Summer Games of Pukatawagan.

The mud pond is another event that takes place before the big events, in the mud pond people wait a hundred meters away from the machine dug pond that is then filled with water by the fire truck and water truck, then volunteers who do not participate go and throw in colorful balls. Each participant stampedes into the mud pond and scatters to find one of the colored balls to win a prize for finding it.

(It is a dirty but fun activity to participant in, but on the good side the community gets together to have fun in the water and mud finding cash prizes.)

Each ball is a certain color representing the amount of money it is worth for finding the ball , the participant then goes the treasure whom pays the participant for finding the ball and the color of the ball will determine the prize for finding it.

Summer Games of Pukatawagan.

The events

The marathon is one of the biggest events of the summer games, most of the community athletes participate in this event and throughout the summer you could see some of the community member practicing or just being in good health. There are girls and boy's marathon and men and women's marathons. the starting point of the marathon takes place at the train station located at mile 99 and ends the youth centre located in the centre of the community. the distance of the marathon is an approximately 21 kilometers.
Paying the winners!

After the long run in the sun the winner are awarded cash prizes for their effort in

Summer Games of Pukatawagan.

running in the marathon. there are 4 prizes there is 1st, 2nd and 3rd for each category.

there are 10 cash prizes given out to the top 10 marathon runners in both men and women category.

The winners are the one that practice each summer season and their effort for their training pays off when they compete in the summer games events and marathon event.

Summer Games of Pukatawagan.

Floor hockey is another event that the community enjoys competing in. The floor hockey tournament is held every year at the local school's gymnasium in the community, the hockey teams gather together in the evening time when all the other events have ended for the day and that's when the floor hockey tournament begins.

There is of course a cash entry to get you and your team to compete in the tournament, but the cash prizes and rush of

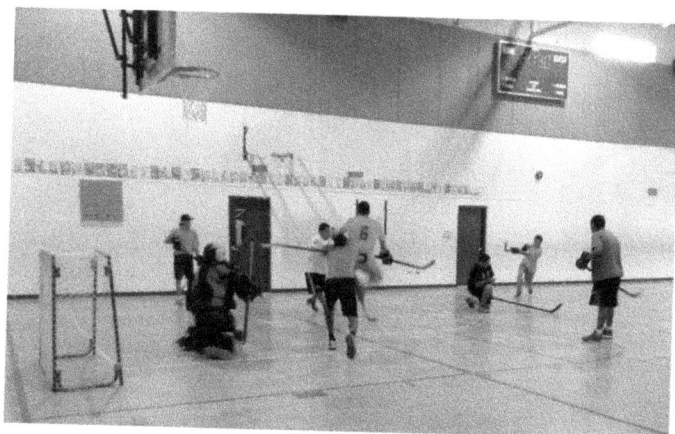

playing seems to be no problem for people who enjoy playing hockey.

Floor hockey is a well known sport in north

Summer Games of Pukatawagan.

America and is the reason for it's popularity in the summer games of pukatawagan. Floor hockey is a fun sport and takes a lot of energy out of the players.

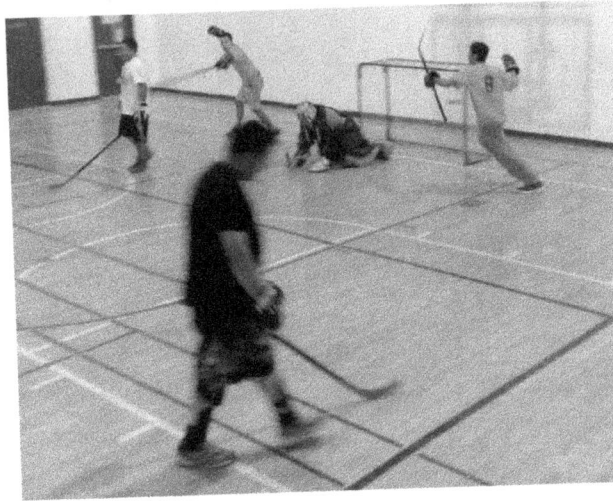

Each team gets the whole year to train in the gymnasium in the evening times when it is open to the community, other sports are played while the gym is open but hockey is one of the community's favorite sport.

After the teams are done competing against each other they shake hands and get together to take a group photo.

Summer Games of Pukatawagan.

Floor Hockey group picture.

BIKE AND RAFT RACE.

The bike race is one of the youth's favorite events, and is held only once during the 3 days of the summer games. There is also a category for women and men during the event. the race takes place at the youth center at noon and they began their starting point in front of the youth centre on the main road and they race each other

to the checkpoint on top of crow rock hill and then race back towards the finish line at the youth centre.

Summer Games of Pukatawagan.

Each participant must provide their own bike to compete in the event and must have brakes for safety reasons. the route they are racing is about 10km long and takes about 5 to 10 minutes to complete the race.

Raft race is a race where community members have to build a raft only using the resources they are allowed with. The race takes place by the lake at sawmill point in the noon time, they start their starting point there and their race towards the finish line by the northern dock. the race is only ½ km long. There is a cash prize for the 3 first rafts to cross the finish line.

The raft race is more of a family event and sometimes each

Summer Games of Pukatawagan.

year they change it the number of people on the raft. Volunteers with boats slowly drive behind the rafts as they race towards the finish line in case of a raft falling apart during the event.

There are also canoe events that take place during the summer games like family canoe race, solo canoe race and voyager race. The small canoe races are about 1km to 10 km long and take up to 10 min to half an hour to complete.

the canoe events take place in the same area as the raft race and start in the morning time around 10:00 am.
each team must provide their own canoe, paddle and life jacket and in case they fall into the water.
The short distance race starts off at the sawmill point and around the cross island and tiger's island. Youth paddle around tiger's island.

The voyage race is a group event and can be either family or friends racing against each other.
there must be 6 paddlers in each voyage canoe and each paddler must have a life jacket and paddle.
The voyage race is usually held on a different date than the other canoe events

There are other events that goes throughout the summer

Summer Games of Pukatawagan.

games and that involve all ages categories so that all ages could compete and also enjoy the hot summer fun. Kids, adults and elders compete in little events like boot throw and neck bone eating, etc.

The little events are held at the youth centre's grounds in the afternoon once the major events like the marathon and canoe races are done in the morning. The youth, adult and elder games are held on the same day by different volunteers.

Kids enjoy playing in the hot sun, adults love watching their children play the events they once participated in and elders enjoy watching their grown children win the events they won and keeping the winning strike in the family. It's a lot of fun to play and enjoy these kind of get together events such as the summer games of Pukatawagan.

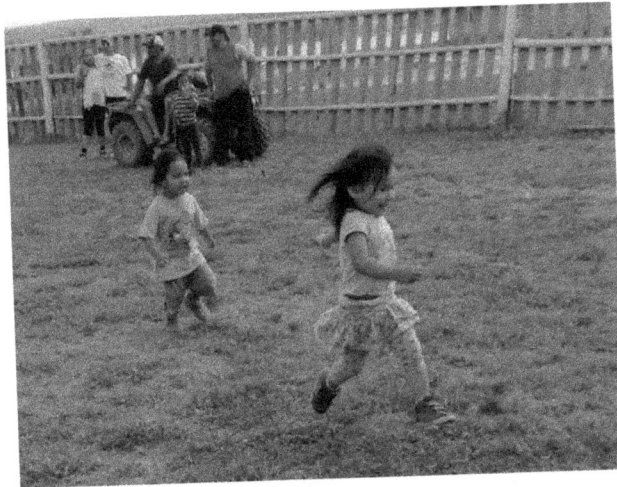

Summer Games of Pukatawagan.

Arts and crafts are apart of the summer games there is paddle and vamp making well those who enjoy doing arts and crafts in the community. it is a fun event to participate in. You get to see all the wonderful colors in the artist's work and if lucky enough purchase one of the art works displayed.

Summer Games of Pukatawagan.

ABOUT THE AUTHOR

Tomy-lee Sinclair is a 23 years old and was born in The Pas Manitoba Canada, and was raised in Pukatawagan, Manitoba, Canada a reservation said and spelled in Cree meaning '' Good Fishing Place''. He got his grade 12 in the local community school called Sakastew School in the year 2016. during Tomy-lee's high school years in Pukatawagan, his favorite subjects were English and history. The most thing he liked about school was the weight room and that there was a wrestling coach. after he graduated he was looking for an opportunity in the community, and he found a few of them, one was work as a radio announcer for Missinipi River Native Communication Incorporated, the 2nd was to be a laborer for Missinipi Construction and the 3rd was to work at the Loon River Lodge Sawmill and the final opportunity was to take the program Community Economic Development, being offered at the local UCN (University of The North) of pukatawagan. His days in Pukatawagan were very active days. Him and his fellow friends would always have something to do with running or challenging each other's strength.